The Earth under your feet

The Earth is made of massive, deep, rocky plates that drift across its surface. In some places, molten rock comes out at the surface and forces the plates apart. In other places, plates collide and one may move under the other. Rocks are being made all the time, worn down and made again. This is called the rock cycle and it doesn't happen overnight, but over millions of years. It was happening even when there were dinosaurs on Earth. All rocks are made of one or more minerals and there are nearly 4,500 minerals in the world. In this book you will see 100 rocks and minerals.

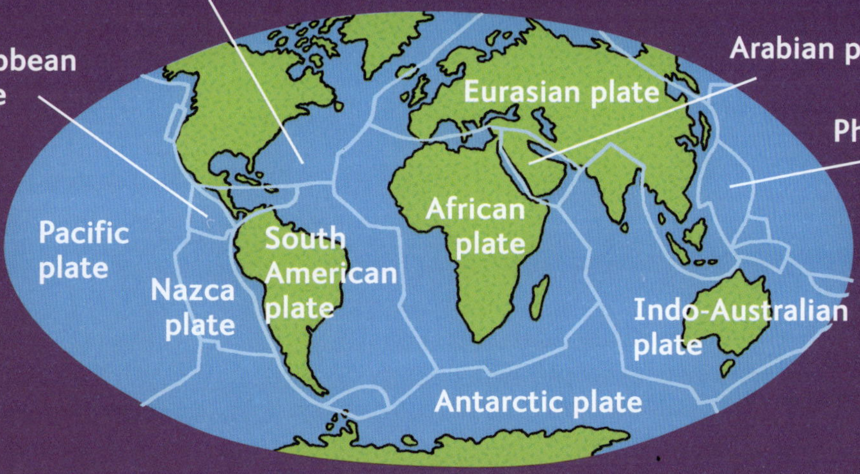

I live on the .... plate

This book belongs to

....

What is a rock and the rock cycle?

There are 3 groups of rocks, igneous, sedimentary and metamorphic.
Match the stickers to the correct outlines.

When the Earth's plates move, this movement squeezes the rocks so hard that the rocks get hot and change. Metamorphic rocks are rocks that were igneous or sedimentary and were changed in this way, Limestone for example is turned into marble.

Deep, deep underground it is so hot that rocks are liquid. When this liquid cools it forms rocks like granite. When a volcano erupts, this liquid rock is forced out of the volcano, cools down and becomes a solid igneous rock. A rock like this is basalt.

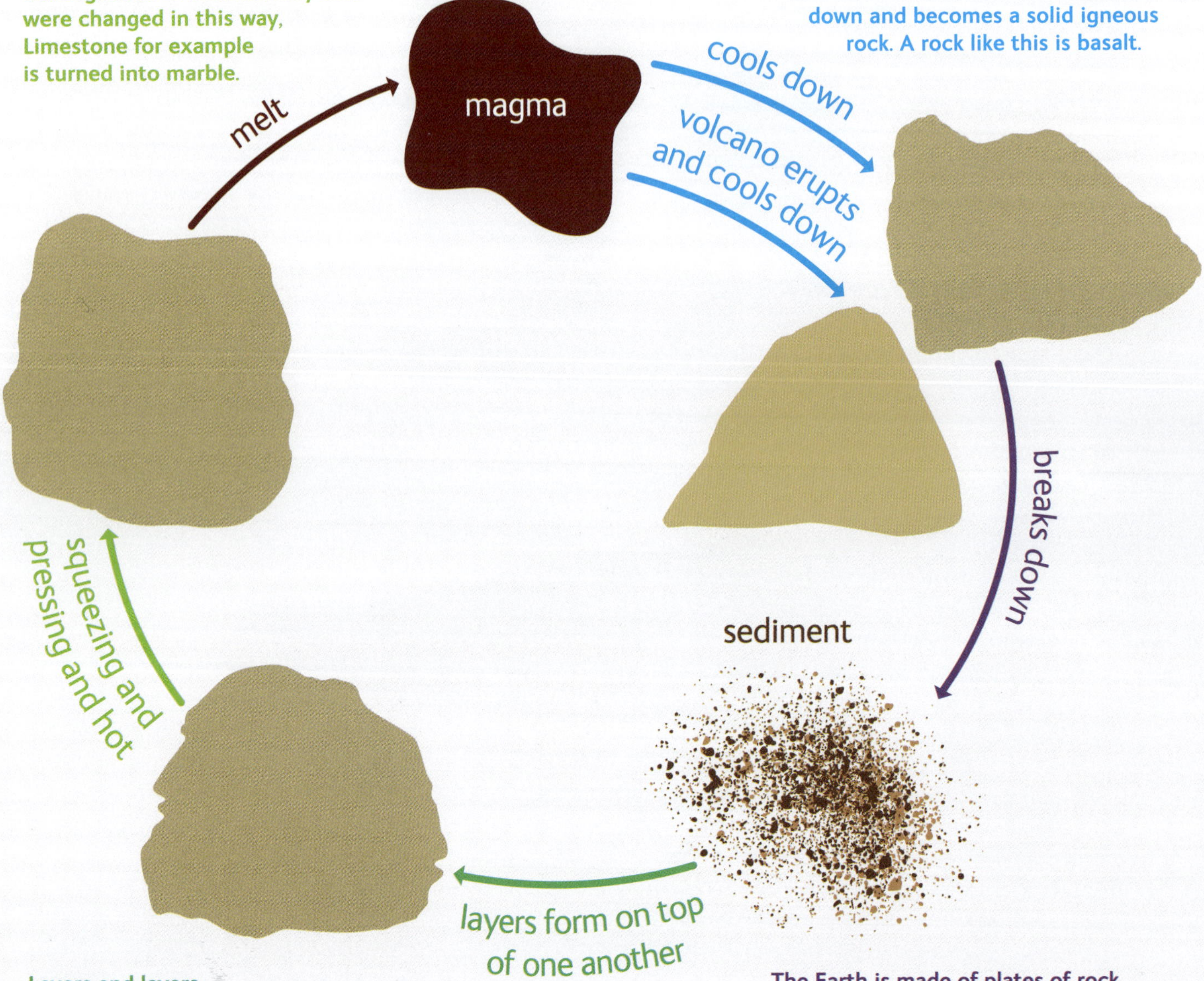

Layers and layers of sediment form on top of one another, pushing down on the sediments underneath and turning it into rock. This is sedimentary rock and sandstone is a rock like this made of sand. Limestone is a sedimentary rock too and is made of the shells of ocean animals that have died.

The Earth is made of plates of rock. When two plates collide they can push upwards, forming tall, jagged mountains. Slowly the sun, rain, wind and snow break down the rock on the mountains. Broken rocks tumble down the mountain and get smaller and smaller. They end up at the bottom of rivers and streams as tiny grains of sediment.

What is a mineral?

So you know what types of rock there are. But what are these rocks made of? A rock is made of one or more minerals. Minerals are formed during those processes that make rocks, such as volcanic eruptions. Minerals are natural and have a structure like a crystal. And we can tell minerals apart because the shape of their crystals are different. Match the stickers to the correct outline.

Gypsum
Gypsum forms from lake water and seawater, and from hot springs and vapours from volcanoes. When the crystals trap grains of sand as they are growing they form what is called a desert rose.

Calcite
Calcite is the most common mineral found in rocks all over the world. It is usually white but it may contain impurities that change it to blue, green or orange. It is found in sedimentary and metamorphic rocks like chalk, limestone and marble.

Pyrite
This mineral looks like the metal gold and is called fool's gold or pyrite.

Aragonite
You might find this mineral on the seashore if you look inside a seashell.

Obsidian
You might find this near a volcano. It is called obsidian, but it is not a mineral as it does not have a crystal structure. It is volcanic glass made when the lava from the volcano cools down.

Snowflake obsidian
This is snowflake obsidian. It is volcanic glass, not a real mineral. Can you see what looks like white snowflakes in the mineral? These are fragments of volcanic ash.

Leopardskin stone
Can you spot the sticker of leopardskin stone? It is cream with black spots.

Thunder-egg agate
This agate forms in spaces produced in volcanic rocks when a volcano explodes. You can tell it's a thunder-egg agate because of the star shape in the middle.

Banded agate
These are banded agates. You can see the layers very clearly like the rings of a cut tree. Some agates are dyed pink and purple to make them look pretty. Can you find the pink banded agate?

Celestine
This mineral is celestine. It is used to make a chemical in fireworks that gives the red colour you see when the firework goes off. Which is strange because the mineral itself is blue!

Diamond
This is the hardest of all the minerals. It is so hard that you can only scratch it with another diamond. It is usually transparent but can be blue, green, pink, yellow and red. Look what happens to it when it is cut and polished.

Chrysocolla
Chrysocolla is a soft mineral and is found wherever there are deposits of the metal copper. Can you find a very bright blue mineral?

Corundum
When some minerals are cut and polished they are called gemstones and are sometimes given a different name. Red corundum is ruby and blue corundum is sapphire.

Malachite
This bright green mineral is called malachite and grows like a bunch of grapes or like a stalagmite.

Extra stickers

Have fun sticking these stickers on the landscape on pages 6 and 7. Where are you most likely to find them, in igneous (I), sedimentary (S) or metamorphic (M) rock, or sometimes all three?

Dolomite (S)

Shark's tooth in olivine (ISM)

Zircon (ISM)

Tiger's eye (M)

Citrine (I)

Opal (S)

Shale (S)

Granite (I)

Turquoise (I)

Labradorite (I)

Lava from Vesuvius (I)

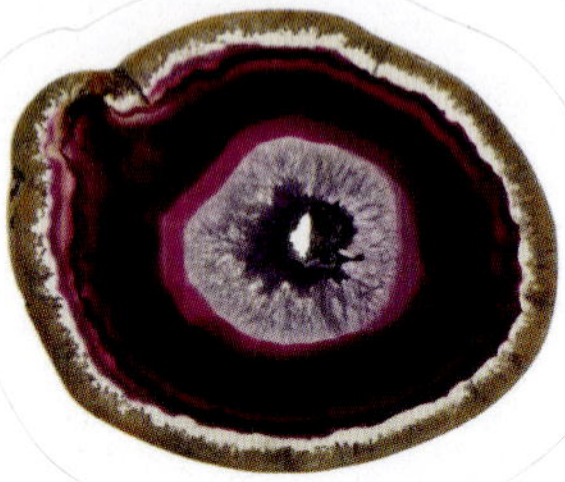

Dyed agate (IS)

Andalusite (M)

Azurite (ISM)

Garnet (M)

Mica (ISM)

Pumice (I)

Moss agate (IS)

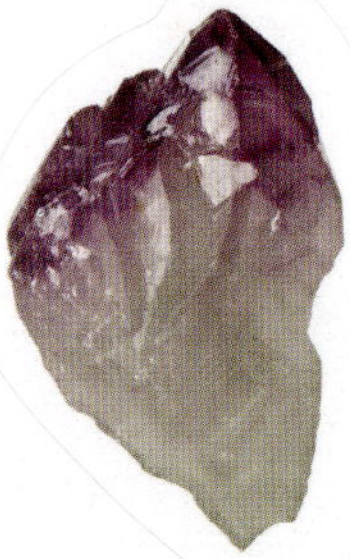

Amethyst (IS)

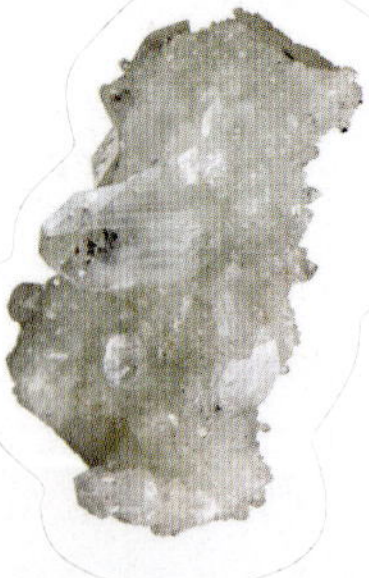

Zeolite (IS)

Pele's hair (I)

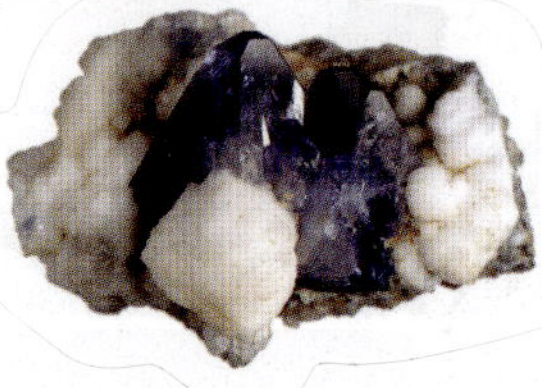

Benitoite (S)

Match the stickers

Peel off and stick these stickers onto the outlines on pages 2, 3, 4 and 5

Chrysocolla

Diamond

Diamond

Hematite

Beryl

Emerald

Jasper

Hematite

Limestone

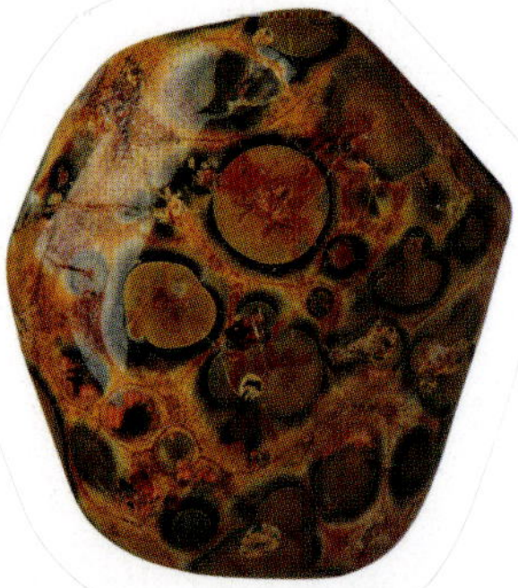

Jasper

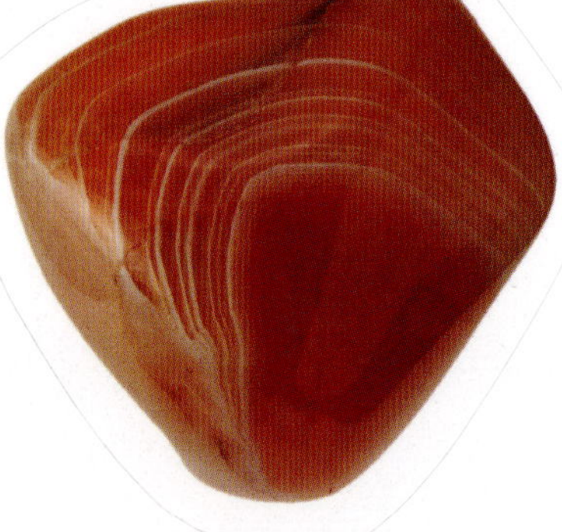

Carnelian

Basalt

Match the stickers

Peel off and stick these stickers onto the outlines on pages 2, 3, 4 and 5

Obsidian

Aragonite

Malachite

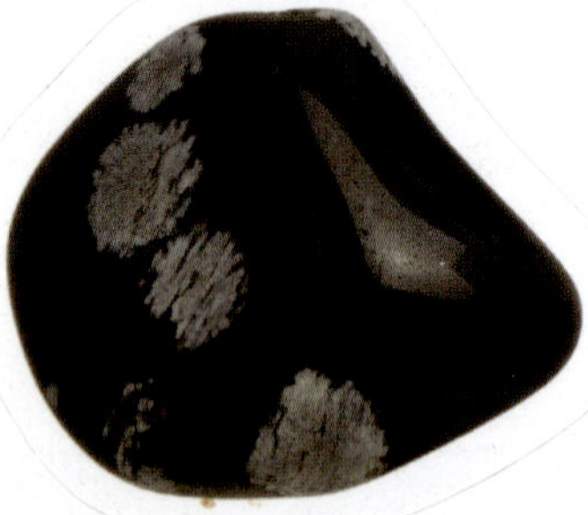

Snowflake obsidian

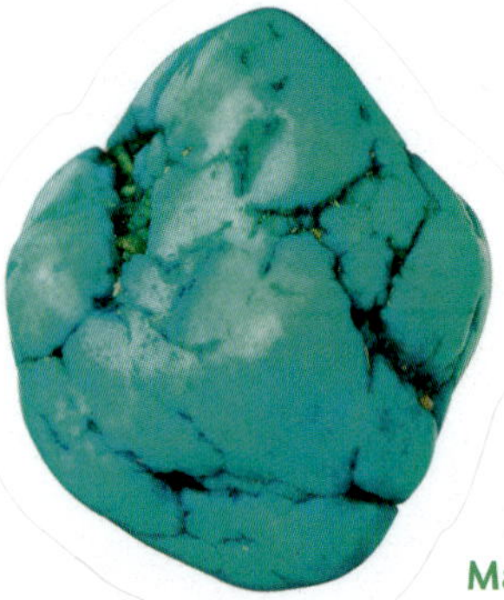

Magnesite

Sulphur

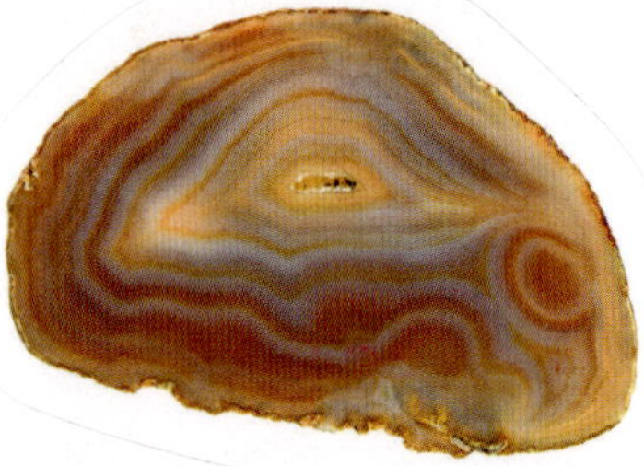

Banded agate

Thunder-egg agate

Pyrite

Dyed banded agate

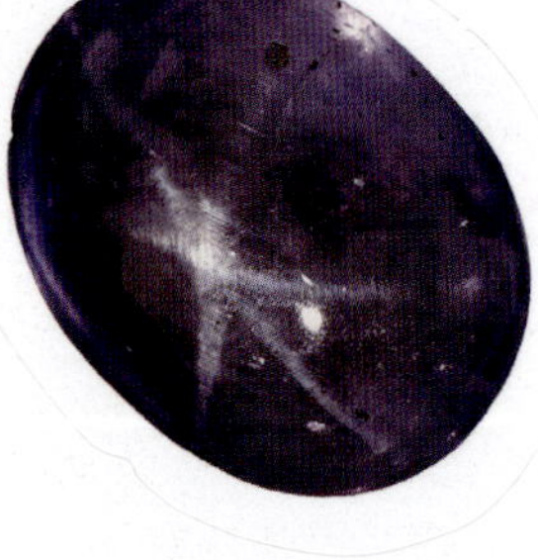

Corundum (sapphire)

Corundum (ruby)

Impure calcite

Impure calcite

Sandstone

Impure calcite

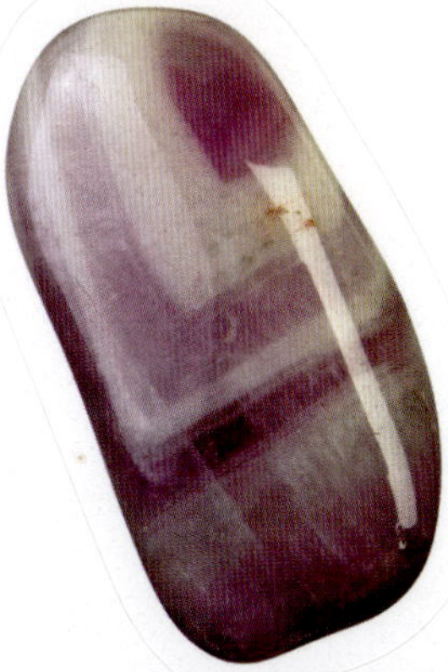

Amethyst

Marble

Celestine

Amethyst

Leopardskin stone

Gypsum

Desert rose

Granite

Extra stickers

Have fun sticking these stickers on the landscape on pages 6 and 7. Where are you most likely to find them, in igneous (I), sedimentary (S) or metamorphic (M) rock, or sometimes all three?

Kimberlite (I)

Granite with tourmaline and quartz (IS)

Slate (M)

Morganite (I)

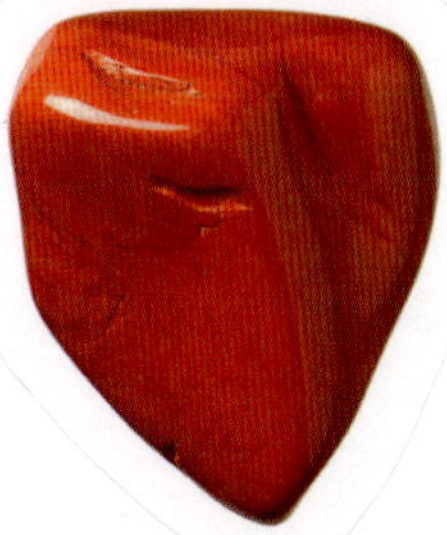

Jasper (M)

Topaz (I)

Pumice (I)

Garnet (ISM)

Pink baryte (S)

Peridot (ISM)

Botswana agate (IS)

Azurite (ISM)

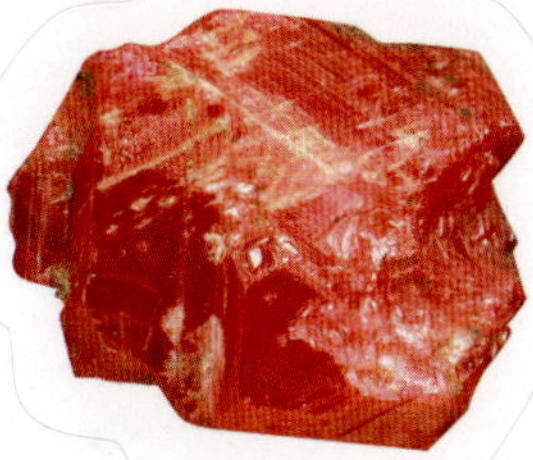

Ruby (M)

Olivine bombs (I)

London clay (S)

Fuchsite (M)

Fluorite (IM)

Unakite (I)

Flint fragment (S)

Peacock ore (ISM)

Chalk (S)

Amethyst (IS)

Rhyolite (I)

Sodalite (I)

Corsite (I)

Amazonite (I)

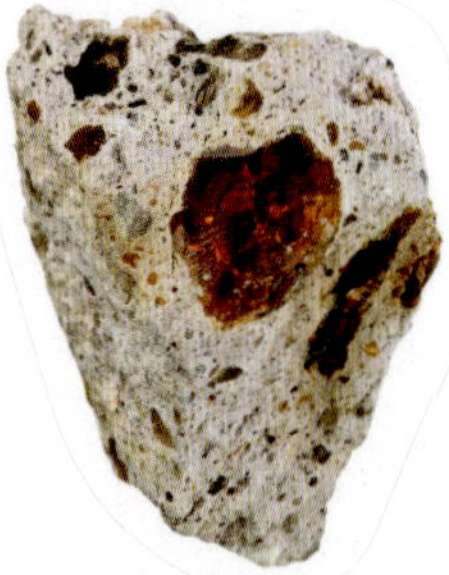
Opal (S)

Tube agate (IS)

Lava (I)

Green quartz (ISM)

Tourmaline (IM)

Turritelle agate (IS)

Padparascha (M)

Chrysoberyl (M)

Cornish granite (IM)

Pyrite (ISM)

Tiger's eye (M)

Chiastolite (M)

Kyanite (M)

Gneiss (M)

Tetrahedrite (ISM)

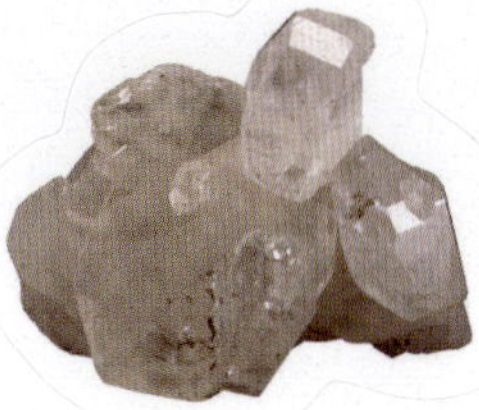
Phenakite (I)

Hematite
Hematite often has a naturally bumpy surface. It comes in opaque shades of red, brown and grey. When it is polished the mineral looks shiny and almost looks like metal. Can you see the two stickers, one is natural and one is polished hematite?

Amethyst
Amethyst is a type of quartz that is purple. A tiny amount of iron in the mineral makes it purple. Crystals of amethyst form in a cluster inside geodes in volcanic rocks.

Carnelian
The name carnelian means 'flesh' in Latin. Can you see why it was given this name? In ancient times it was used to make seal rings for sealing letters with hot wax, because hot wax does not stick to carnelian.

Magnesite
Magnesite is a translucent mineral that is easy to break. It is white or colourless but it is often dyed so that it looks like another expensive mineral called turquoise.

Sulphur
Sulphur is bright yellow and forms in hot springs and volcanic craters. Sometimes sulphur gives off a horrible gas that smells like rotten eggs.

Jasper
Jasper is made up of a lot of tiny quartz crystals all packed together. It is found in nearly any colour. The red and brown jaspers have iron in them and may be patterned.

Beryl
Beryl forms in hexagonal crystals and produces some of the most rare and valuable gemstones. The deep green transparent variety of beryl is emerald.

Your own rock world

Use the extra stickers to fill in your world with rocks and minerals. Remember some rocks and minerals are found in the mountains, some near rivers and some under the sea.

Colour in the minerals

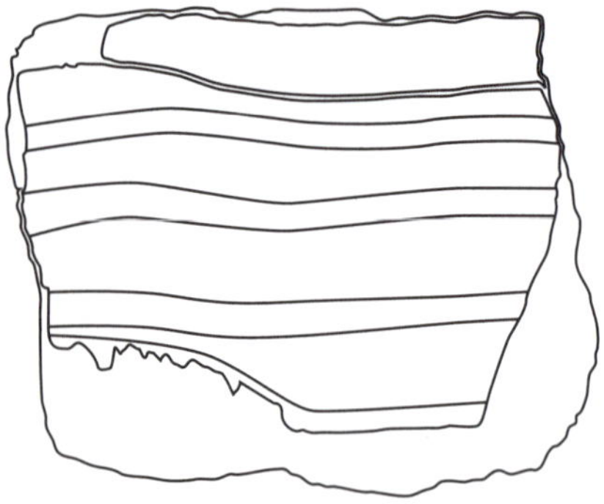

Tiger's eye

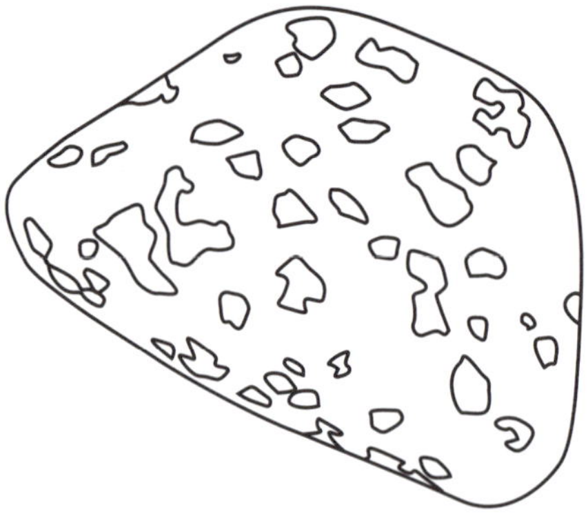

Leopardskin stone

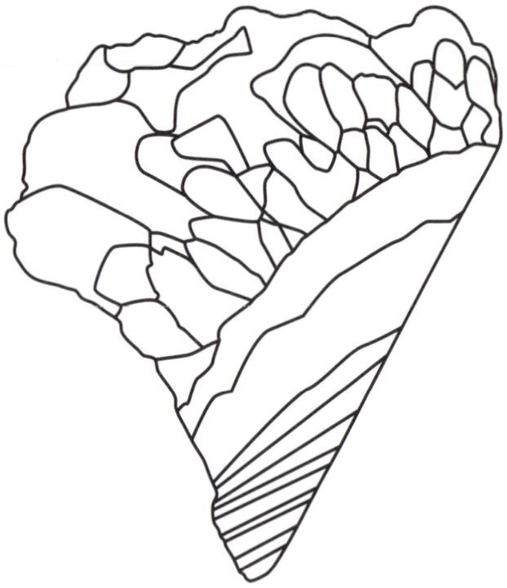

Malachite

What comes from where?

See if you can find...

5 diamonds
2 emeralds
1 amethyst
2 rubies
3 sapphires